Cooking

with

THE HUNGRY MONK

by

Ian Dowding

Nigel and Susan Mackenzie

HUNGRY MONK PUBLICATIONS
Jevington
Near Polegate
Sussex

Also in the same series:—

The Secrets of the Hungry Monk
The Deeper Secrets of the Hungry Monk
The Hungry Monk at Home
The Secret Sauce Book of the Hungry Monk

*We would like to thank M. et
Mme. Jo Bernard of the
Auberge du Vert for their
wonderful hospitality.*

First published December 1983

Ferme Auberge du Vert,
Wierre – Effroy,
62250 Marquise
France

There was a time when to talk about 'English Cooking' was to invite laughter and scorn. Although we had the best raw materials of almost anywhere in Europe we had a reputation for ruining most of them.

Lamb was so often roasted without garlic or rosemary till grey, Fish and Vegetables boiled to a watery death, Duck served soggy-skinned and greasy and so on.

When we opened The Hungry Monk in 1968 we didn't know anything about running a Restaurant and even less about cooking for numbers – we did however have a clear idea of the style of food we wanted to serve. It had to be not only imaginative and exciting but able to do justice in flavour and texture to the wonderful raw materials at our disposal. None of which we would have had the slightest chance of achieving had it not been for our enormous luck in meeting Ian Dowding – then aged 19 – who agreed to be our first Chef. Thanks to his enthusiasm and dedication we managed to go some way towards translating these ambitions in to our own style of cooking.

Our first cookery book The Secrets of The Hungry Monk, written in 1971 was primarily for our own use as a kind of kitchen manual. We certainly never envisaged that the book would sell many copies and even less did we dare to imagine that in 1983 Ian would still be with us. It is therefore a joy and a privilege to find ourselves once again sitting round a table in this utterly delightful Auberge writing a sequel.

'Cooking with The Hungry Monk' embodies many of the lessons and discoveries that inevitably emerge from a Kitchen that has been cooking a different menu almost every day for sixteen years. The book is full of delicious dishes that we know have given pleasure to countless customers. In every case we believe we have found the simplest and most fool-proof methods of preparation which we have tried to express in the plainest English.

N.A.M.

CONTENTS

CONTENTS (cont.)

CONTENTS (cont.)

STARTERS

CHILLED PRAWN and AVOCADO SOUP

A Summer soup and a welcome reworking of that most popular of combinations Avocado and Prawns.

To serve 4

2 ripe avocados
8fl oz/225ml natural yoghurt
½pt/300ml milk
8oz/225grms peeled prawns
4 tablespoonfuls of double cream
the juice of ¼ of a lemon
chopped chives
a shake of tabasco
salt

Preparation
Peel and stone the avocados

Method
This can only be made just before it is to be eaten otherwise the avocados will discolour. A liquidiser makes life a great deal easier as it is necessary to start by pureéing the avocados with the yoghurt, milk and salt, followed by the tabasco and lemon juice.

This is the basic soup and can now be poured in to the four bowls. Decorate by sprinkling the prawns on the top followed by a spoonful of double cream and a generous pinch of chopped chives.

Serve with hot granary bread.

JERUSALEM ARTICHOKE SOUP

This is a delicious soup and delightfully simple to make.

To serve 4-6

1lb/450grms Jerusalem artichokes
3oz/75grms onion
½pt/300ml chicken stock
¾pt/450ml milk
1oz/25grms butter
1oz/25grms plain flour
¼pt/150ml double cream
salt and white pepper

Preparation
Scrub the artichokes to remove the skin. Cut away any blemishes. Cut the artichokes in to thick slices. Chop the onion.

Method
Take a large pan and bring to the boil the artichokes and onion in the stock with the milk and seasoning. Simmer until the vegetables are tender. Pass everything through a sieve or liquidise.

In a separate large pan melt the butter, stir in the flour and gradually add the vegetable puree, stirring all the time. Bring to the boil, whisk in the cream, adjust the seasoning and serve with hot granary bread.

CREAM CHEESE and FRESH HERB QUICHE

To serve 8

THE QUICHE

12oz/350 grms shortcrust pastry,
see page 92
8oz/225grms cream cheese
8oz/225grms cottage cheese
3 eggs
$\frac{1}{2}$pt/300 ml single cream
3 heaped tablespoons of chopped
fresh herbs which must include
parsley and chives as well as any
or all of the following: rosemary,
basil, oregano, sorrel
the juice of a lemon,
salt and freshly ground
black pepper

TOMATO SAUCE

10 ripe tomatoes
2oz/50grms butter
salt and freshly ground
black pepper

Equipment A flan tin – 10in diameter x 1$\frac{1}{2}$ in deep.

Preparation

Preheat the over to No. 4/350 degrees. Line the flan tin with the pastry, prick all over with a fork and bake blind in the top of the oven until just crisp.

Method

This is one of the simplest quiches to make particularly if you are fortunate enough to have a good liquidiser.

Simply combine the cream cheese, cottage cheese, eggs, cream, herbs, lemon juice and seasoning in a bowl and beat to a smooth consistency. Pour the mixture in to the waiting pastry case and bake in the middle of the oven for 25-35 minutes until firm to the touch.

While the quiche is baking you have time to make the tomato sauce by stewing all the ingredients in a heavy based pan until the tomatoes are soft. Pass the mixture through a fine sieve and keep it hot.

Serve the quiche just warm and hand the sauce separately.

FEUILLETAGE of CHEESE with MUSTARD SAUCE

Crisp pastry parcels filled with a mixture of melted cheese.

To serve 6

6oz/175grms Philadelphia
cream cheese
3oz/75grms good Cheddar cheese
3oz/75grms mild blue cheese
1 egg yolk
1 tablespoonful of freshly chopped
herbs (parsley, sage and chives)
a clove of garlic
freshly ground black pepper

12oz/350grms puff pastry
1 egg
$\frac{1}{2}$ cup of milk
vegetable oil

THE MUSTARD SAUCE
1 teaspoonful of Moutard
de Meaux
$\frac{1}{4}$pt/150ml double cream
$\frac{1}{4}$pt/150ml Hollandaise Sauce,
see page 90

Preparation
Preheat the oven to No. 7/425 degrees.
Crush the garlic with a little salt.
Beat the egg in to the milk for the egg wash
Oil a baking sheet

Method
Grate the cheddar and the blue cheese and beat together with the cream cheese, egg yolk, herbs, garlic and black pepper. Roll out the puff pastry in to six rectangles and divide the cheese mixture in to a heap in the centre of each leaving a good border of uncovered pastry on all four sides which should be brushed with the egg wash.

Our aim is to make these in to neat parcels by bringing the two short sides over the top allowing a generous overlap. Finish by crimping both ends to create a perfect seal so that as the cheese melts, none escapes.

Brush with egg wash and place in the top of the oven for 10-15 minutes until golden.

While these are baking we can make the sauce. This is quite simply Meaux mustard and double cream stirred together over a low heat before lifting off and combining with the Hollandaise sauce.

Serve by surrounding each feuilletage with the sauce and decorate with a little greenery.

GLOBE ARTICHOKE STUFFED with PRAWNS and PEPPERS

To serve 4

4 large Globe Artichokes – Brittany Prince are best
8oz/225grms prawns – peeled and drained
4oz/100grms green and red peppers
8fl oz/200ml home-made Mayonnaise, see page 91

Preparation
Finely chop the green and red peppers. Put a large saucepan of salted water on to boil. Cut the stalks off the artichokes level with the base and cut the top off a good third of the way down. Trim off the tips of the other leaves with scissors.

Method
Immerse the artichokes in the boiling water and cook for anything up to 45 minutes depending on size (test with a skewer in to the base).

Once cooked remove and place upside down on a tray to drain and cool. This is a good moment to make the filling which is simply a matter of combining the prawns, chopped peppers and the Mayonnaise.

To stuff the artichokes, remove the little leaves in the centre together with the choke (the fine hairs that grow up the centre from the base). Spoon in the filling and serve.

MUSHROOMS in CAFE de PARIS BUTTER

Field mushrooms in garlicky butter
with a hint of anchovy

To serve 4

1lb 8oz/675 grms field or cultivated flat mushrooms – not button or cup mushrooms
4oz/100grms butter
4 anchovy fillets
1 clove of garlic
1 tablespoonful of finely chopped parsley
1 tablespoonful of vegetable oil
$\frac{1}{8}$pt/75ml water
salt and freshly ground black pepper

Preparation
Wipe the mushrooms and trim the stalks. pureé the anchovies. Crush the garlic with a little salt.

Method
Take a covered pan and poach the mushrooms until soft in the water with the oil and salt. This will produce some good stock that will later be amalgamated with the melted butter.

Turning our attention to the Café de Paris butter, this is made by combining the garlic, anchovy, parsley and black pepper with the butter and melting in a heavy based pan before introducing the cooked mushrooms together with four tablespoonfuls of the stock. Shake and stir over a high heat until the butter and stock come together to produce a sauce.

Serve immediately with hot French bread.

DEVILLED CRAB

Little pots of crabmeat in a hot piquant sauce.

To serve 4-6

12oz/350grms white crabmeat	2 tablespoonfuls of double cream
2oz/50grms onion	1 egg
2oz/50grms button mushrooms	the juice of half a lemon
2oz/50grms celery	1 level teaspoonful of prepared
a clove of garlic	English mustard
$\frac{1}{2}$ teaspoonful of freshly	1 tablespoonful of white wine
chopped thyme	vinegar
1oz/25grms butter	3 shakes of tabasco
1oz/25grms flour	salt and freshly ground black
8fl oz/225ml fish stock	pepper

Preparation

Either buy just the crab claws or frozen white crab meat. As frozen crabmeat
has a high water content a 1lb pack will yield 12oz/350grms of meat. It is
better to squeeze it gently rather than just drain it. Use this liquor as part of your
fish stock.
Hard boil the egg, cool, peel and chop.
Finely chop the onion, celery and mushrooms.
Crush the garlic with a little salt.

Method

Melt the butter in a heavy based pan and fry the onions, celery, mushrooms,
garlic and thyme until soft without colouring. Stir in the flour, cook for a
moment before gradually adding the fish stock, lemon juice, tabasco, mustard
and vinegar to make a smooth sauce.

Now tip in the crabmeat and chopped egg. Heat through and adjust the
seasoning, adding more tabasco if that is your taste. Finish by stirring in the
cream.

Light the grill. Spoon the the mixture in to ramekins, sprinkle with parmesan
cheese and brown under the grill before serving with hot garlic bread.

POTTED CRAB

An elegant but simple treatment for making the most of fresh crabmeat.

To serve 8-10

1lb/450grms fresh or frozen crabmeat
12oz/350grms cream cheese
4oz/100grms butter
The juice of 1½ lemons
1 tablespoonful of chopped parsley
a clove of garlic
a dash of tabasco
grated nutmeg
salt and freshly ground black pepper

Preparation
Crush the garlic with a little salt. Soften the butter. If using frozen crabmeat squeeze out the excess water from the white meat.

Method
Ideally one wants this dish to be fairly light and airy to stop it being too rich. This is best achieved by first beating the butter and cream cheese together and then whipping in all the other ingredients except the crabmeat until the mixture becomes fluffy. Only then should you fold in the crabmeat and spoon in to individual ramekins or a paté dish.

Decorate with watercress and lemon. Serve with crunchy brown toast.

MUSSEL TART

We first ate this tart in Normandy having missed the ferry home. The memory of this delicious dish has lingered long after the inconvenience was forgotten!

To serve 6

12oz/350grms shortcrust pastry, see page 92
60 mussels – approximately 3pts/1.5 litres
$\frac{1}{4}$pt/150ml dry white wine
2 eggs
$\frac{1}{4}$pt/150ml double cream
a small onion
the juice of $\frac{1}{2}$ a lemon
a pinch of fresh chervil
freshly ground black pepper

Equipment 6 flan tins – 4in. diameter x $\frac{3}{4}$in. deep.

Preparation
Preheat the oven to No. 5/375 degrees. Line the flan tins with the pastry, prick all over with a fork and bake blind until crisp and golden. Finely dice the onion and divide in half.

Clean the mussels by rinsing under plenty of cold water. Remove the beards and discard any with open or damaged shells. Take a large pan and pour in the wine, lemon juice, half the chopped onion together with the mussels. Cover tightly and bring to the boil, shaking the pan from time to time. After about 5 minutes the mussels should all be open. Drain and reserve the stock discarding any unopened shells. Allow the mussels to cool.

Method
Remove the mussels from their shells and distribute evenly across the bases of the flans. Sprinkle over the remaining onion. There will be a certain amount of gritty sediment in the mussel stock and this should be strained out before reducing the liquor back to $\frac{1}{4}$pt/150ml.

Allow this liquor to cool slightly before whisking in the double cream and eggs. Toss in the chervil and season with black pepper. All that remains is to pour this sauce over the mussels and bake the tarts for between 25 and 35 minutes in the centre of the oven.

Serve piping hot with wedges of lemon and cayenne pepper.

PRAWN, CRAB and SMOKED SALMON ROULADE

A fish soufflé filled with seafood and rolled up like a Swiss roll.

To serve 10-12

ROULADE BASE
1lb/450grms plaice or lemon sole –
filleted and skinned
4 eggs
¼pt/150ml double cream
grated nutmeg
salt and freshly ground
black pepper

FILLING
10oz/250grms peeled prawns
(well drained if using frozen)

10oz/250grms white crabmeat
(well drained if using frozen)
4oz/100grms sliced
smoked salmon
1 tablespoonful of
chopped parsley
1 tablespoonful of chopped
canned pimentos
½pt/300ml thick Mayonnaise,
see page 91

Equipment A shallow baking tray 16in. x 12 in. or two 8in. x 12in. (if you have a small oven).

Preparation
Preheat the oven to No. 8/450 degrees. Separate the eggs. Cut a piece of greaseproof paper that is large enough to exactly cover the base and sides of the baking tray. As we need to oil both sides of this paper the best way is to oil the tray itself and then press first one side of the paper in to place, lift it off, turn it over and press the other side down.

Method
Firstly poach the fish in some salted water, drain well and allow to cool. (This should yield approximately 8oz/225grms cooked fish.) Transfer the fish to a liquidiser and pureé with the egg yolks, nutmeg and seasoning. Whip the egg whites in a large bowl until stiff, fold in the fish pureé and the cream. The mixture is now ready to be poured on to the greaseproof paper and spread with a palette knife to an even thickness from corner to corner. Place on the top shelf of the oven for 10-15 minutes until golden. Allow to cool.

The Filling
Mix together the prawns, crabmeat, pimentos, parsley and mayonnaise.

Assembly

The idea is to end up with something that looks like a Swiss roll. Firstly we must remove the greaseproof paper and this is best done by gently placing the base face down on a fresh piece of paper and easing off the greaseproof, starting at the corners and side edges. Great care must be taken here as it is only too easy to tear the base which will make rolling up with the filling inside very difficult.

The next task is to cover the base first with slices of smoked salmon and then an even spread of the fish and mayonnaise mixture. Because the whole thing is about to be rolled it makes life very much easier if the mixture is not spread down a 1 inch border at the beginning of the roll and again at the end.

Now starting with the uncovered border furthest away from you, gently roll the base up towards you using the greaseproof paper to give even support. Allow to stand in the fridge for about 2 hrs. Carve in thick slices. This dish is at its best eaten the same day that it is made.

QUENELLES au GRATIN

It is hard to describe a quenelle as it is lighter than a dumpling but creamier than a souffle. Either way they are delicious and bring out the full delicate flavour of fish.

To serve 8

THE QUENELLES
1lb/450 grms salmon, turbot or
pike – filleted and skinned (retain
the skin and bones for stock)
½pt/300ml water
4oz/100grms plain flour
2oz/50grms butter
2 eggs
2 egg whites
2 tablespoonfuls of double cream

grated parmesan cheese
salt and white pepper
grated nutmeg

THE SAUCE
1pt/600ml Bechamel sauce,
see page 87
¼pt/150ml fish stock
1 glass of dry white wine
½pt/300ml whipping cream

Equipment A shallow ovenproof dish approximately 3½pts/2 litres capacity
A piping bag

Preparation
Poach the fish skin and bones in enough water and wine to cover. Drain in to another saucepan and reduce the liquor to ¼pt/150ml.

Method
THE QUENELLES
We start by making a paste by heating the water and butter together until the butter is melted, followed by stirring in the flour and beating over the heat for a minute. Allow to cool thoroughly.
Turning our attention to the raw fish, this must be made in to a smooth pureé either by putting it in a liquidiser or passing it through a mincer twice.
Back to the paste which should have sufficiently cooled by now to gradually beat in the eggs and extra egg whites until smooth and glossy. Fold in the fish and cream, nutmeg and seasoning. Place in the fridge to chill.

THE SAUCE
Approximately 1¼hrs. before you plan to serve the quenelles light the oven at No. 4/350 degrees. Heat the Bechamel sauce together with the fish stock. Then add the cream, bring to the boil and pour in to the ovenproof dish.

Assembly

Take the quenelle mixture from the fridge and transfer in to a piping bag without its nozzle.

The idea is to extrude quenelles of approximately 2 inches long each straight in to the shallow dish of hot sauce. (Alternatively they can be shaped between two dessert spoons dipped in hot water.) Cover with foil and bake in the centre of the oven for 30-40 minutes so that the quenelles are puffed up and firm to the touch. Sprinkle with parmesan and brown under a hot grill. Serve immediately.

Variations

Prawns can be added to the sauce at the last moment just before grilling. Quenelles are delicious eaten on their own with a little salad or plain watercress. Alternatively they can be used as an accompaniment to fish.

SALMON MOUSSELINE PANCAKES

A crisp pancake filled with salmon mousseline and served hot with prawn sauce. Equally suitable as either a starter or main course.

To serve 8

THE MOUSSELINE
1lb/450grms fresh salmon –
filleted
4 egg whites
1pt/600ml double cream
grated nutmeg
salt and white pepper

8 pancakes, see page 93
melted butter

THE SAUCE
½pt/300ml Bechamel sauce,
see page 87
½pt/300ml double cream
8oz/225grms button mushrooms
4oz/100grms peeled prawns
2oz/50grams butter
4fl oz/100ml dry white wine
the juice of ½ a lemon
a small clove of garlic
salt and freshly ground
black pepper

Equipment A liquidiser
A baking tray 16in. x 12in. or two 8in. x 12in. (if your oven is small)

Preparation
Wipe and slice the mushrooms. Crush the garlic with a little salt. Grease the baking tray. Preheat the oven to No. 7/425 degrees

Method
To make Salmon Mousseline a Magimix or something like it is an essential piece of equipment.

One starts by liquidising the raw fish with the nutmeg, salt and pepper. Stop the machine and add in the egg whites. Give it another burst. Stop the machine and pour in the cream before giving a final burst just long enough to make the whole mixture smooth and creamy. Transfer in to a bowl and allow to stand in the fridge for at least 3hrs. to give sufficient time for the mousseline to become firm.

The Sauce
Melt the butter in a heavy based sauté pan. Cook the mushrooms and the garlic until soft but not coloured. Next add the lemon juice, wine and seasoning. Bring to the boil before pouring in the Bechamel and the double cream. Bring to the boil again. Remove from the heat and toss in the peeled prawns. Correct the seasoning and set aside.

Assembly

We want to make each pancake in to a parcel with one eighth of the mousseline mixture in the middle and the four sides brought over to cover it.

Place the pancake parcel, folds downwards on the greased baking tray and brush the smooth top with melted butter. Bake in the middle of the oven for 15 minutes until the pancake has puffed up a little and become crisp and golden.

Finally serve by surrounding each pancake with the prawn sauce.

SCALLOPS MOUSSELINE TERRINE

A very pretty mousseline with a marvellously delicate flavour.

To serve 8

1lb 8oz/675grms trimmed and
drained scallops
2oz/50grms raw salmon fillet

¾pt/450ml double cream
3 egg whites
salt, white pepper and nutmeg

Equipment A 2¾pt/1.6 litres to 3pt/1.8 litres capacity oblong terrine dish or
loaf tin

Preparation

Preheat the oven to No. 3½/350 degrees.
Take the scallops and separate the white from the coral meat.
Line the bottom of the terrine with lightly oiled greaseproof paper.

Method

What makes this dish so attractive is that the coral and white colour scheme of
a fresh scallop is re-created in the mousseline. To achieve this effect we must
make two separate mousselines.

Starting with the white meat this should be liquidised with two of the egg
whites and seasoning until smooth and then liquidised again with ½pt of the
cream until glossy. Transfer to a bowl. Wash out the liquidiser and repeat the
process this time using the coral meat of the scallops, the salmon fillet,
seasoning and the remaining egg white and cream.

We are now ready to assemble the terrine. Scoop just over half the white
mousseline in to the terrine and with a spoon make a deep trough. In to this
carefully position the coral mousseline making sure that the mixture lies only in
the middle. End by spooning the remaining white mixture around the coral core.
Cover the terrine.

Position in the centre of a roasting tray filled with 2in. of hot water before
covering the whole works with foil and sealing round the edges of the roasting
tray. Place in the centre of the oven for one hour.

Remove from the oven and allow to cool. Chill in the fridge overnight and turn
out on to a flat serving dish having first run a thin knife round the sides. Peel off
the greaseproof and serve in ½in. thick slices. If all has gone according to plan
you should be rewarded with the reassuring sight of a white scallop terrine with
a perfect round of coral bang in the middle!

Accompany the terrine with watercress and soured cream spiced with cayenne
alongside a dollop of redcurrant jelly.

SMOKED MACKEREL PATE

To serve 6

1lb/450grms smoked mackerel fillets
4oz/100grms butter
3 tablespoonfuls of natural yoghurt
the juice of a lemon
2 tablespoonfuls of chopped parsley
½ teaspoonful of ground coriander
freshly ground black pepper

Preparation
Skin the mackerel fillets. Melt the butter.

Method
This is very simple to prepare. If you like a fairly rough texture then simply mash up the mackerel fillets with all the other ingredients and transfer in to individual ramekins to serve with wedges of lemon and either hot bread or toast.

A smoother texture can be achieved by using a liquidiser.

SMOKED SALMON QUICHE

To serve 8

14oz/400grms brown pastry, see page 92
12oz/350grms smoked salmon trimmings
¾pt/450ml milk
½pt/300ml single cream
3 eggs
2oz/50grms butter
½ Spanish onion
the juice of a lemon
2 cloves
a bay leaf
freshly ground black pepper

Equipment A flan tin – 10in. diameter x 1½in. deep.

Preparation
Preheat the oven to No. 5/375 degrees. Line the flan tin with the pastry, prick all over with a fork and bake blind. Slice up the smoked salmon in to ½in. strips and soak in ½pt/300ml of the milk for at least half an hour to remove some of the salt. Drain, rinse and pat the fish dry.

Whisk together the eggs, cream, the rest of the milk, lemon juice and black pepper. Dice the onion finely.

Method
Melt the butter in a pan and lightly saute the onion and smoked salmon, together with the cloves and bay leaf until all the ingredients are well coated with the butter. Spoon this mixture in to the waiting pastry case and then pour over the egg and cream mixture.

Return to the oven and bake for a further 30-40 minutes until just golden brown and firm to the touch. Serve warm with watercress salad.

SQUID STEW with ROUILLE

Fresh squid stewed in a rich creamy sauce accompanied by a dollop of peppery rouille.

To serve 4

THE STEW

1lb/450grms fresh large squid
4oz/100grms onion
4oz/100grms button mushrooms
10oz/275grms tinned tomatoes
including the juice
1 small green pepper
2 cloves of garlic
$\frac{1}{2}$pt/300ml Bechamel sauce,
see page 87
5fl oz/125ml dry white wine

2fl oz/50ml single cream
2fl oz/50ml vegetable oil
1 dessertspoonful of white
wine vinegar
$\frac{1}{2}$ teaspoonful of Herbes
de Provence
$\frac{1}{2}$ teaspoonful of prepared
English mustard
2 shakes of tabasco
salt

Preparation

The price one pays for the pleasure of eating fresh squid is preparing it. A job that should be done on the draining board of your sink. Start by cutting off all the tentacles by the head and set to one side. Next grasp the head firmly and pull steadily away from the body. Unless you are very unlucky all the entrails will come too and the whole lot can be dumped. Remove the spine which appears to be made of clear plastic and wash the body inside and out. Peel off and discard the skin. Cut off the fins and slice in to thin strips. Cut the body in to rings about $\frac{1}{4}$in. thick. Finally chop up the two long tentacles.
Peel and slice the onion. De-seed and slice the pepper. Wipe and slice the mushrooms. Crush the garlic with a little salt. Chop the tinned tomatoes and reserve the juice.

Method

Take a saucepan large enough to accommodate all the ingredients and commence by cooking the onion, pepper, mushrooms, garlic and herbs in the vegetable oil until they are soft. Add the squid and cook until it becomes opaque. Now tip in the tomatoes, white wine, mustard, vinegar, tabasco and seasoning. Bring to the boil, add the Bechamel and cook for 30 minutes. Finish by stirring in the cream. Adjust the seasoning.

THE ROUILLE

1x7oz/200grms tin of red pimentos
1$\frac{1}{2}$ oz/40grms stale white bread
without the crusts
2 tablespoonfuls of olive oil

the juice of $\frac{1}{4}$ of a lemon
2 cloves of a garlic
$\frac{1}{4}$ of a level teaspoonful of cayenne
salt

Method

Drain the pimentos. Gently fry the garlic in the oil until soft but not coloured. Now tip all the ingredients in to a liquidiser and pulverise to a thick pureé.

To serve

Nothing could be simpler. Just heat the stew, ladle in to fairly deep bowls and hand round the rouille.

CHICKEN CREAM and SHERRY PATE

A smooth creamy paté

To serve 6-8

1lb/450grms chicken livers
8oz/225grms butter
4oz/100grms smoked bacon
4oz/100grms cream cheese
3fl oz/75ml double cream
2fl oz/50ml dry sherry
1 measure of brandy
2 cloves of garlic
1 teaspoonful of chopped fresh herbs
(rosemary, thyme and sage) or a pinch of mixed dried herbs
salt and freshly ground black pepper

Preparation
Cut up the bacon. Crush the garlic with a little salt.

Method
Firstly we need to cook the chicken livers, bacon, garlic, herbs, salt and pepper in a shallow pan in 6oz/150grms of the butter. Once this is done the pan can be removed from the heat and allowed to cool slightly. Stir in the cream, sherry and brandy and transfer to a liquidiser with the cream cheese. Liquidise to a consistency that may seem worryingly runny but will in fact set firm if left to cool in the fridge either in individual ramekins or in a pate dish.

In either case seal the surface by melting the two remaining ounces of the butter and pouring over the top. Serve with fresh bread, thickly cut and toasted.

HAM STUFFED with MUSHROOMS and GRUYERE

Crisp parcels of ham.

To serve 6

6 large slices of ham
6 large flat or field mushrooms
6oz/175grms grated gruyere
a little Kirsch
freshly ground black pepper
plain flour
1 egg
½ cup of milk
8oz/225grms breadcrumbs, see page 93
vegetable oil

Preparation
Wipe the mushroom and remove the stalks.
Mixed the grated gruyere with a little kirsch and black pepper.
In a shallow dish beat the egg in to the milk to make the egg wash.

Method
Fry the mushrooms in a little oil until soft. Drain and cool.
Lay out the six slices of ham on a board and place the mushrooms, underside up, on one half of each slice. Distribute the cheese mixture evenly on to each mushroom and fold the ham over to cover. Carefully pat with flour all over. Dip in to the egg wash followed by a dip in to the breadcrumbs to achieve a liberal coating.
These are now ready for frying in ½ inch of oil in a shallow pan turning once, until golden. Lift out and drain for a moment on some kitchen towel.
Serve with wedges of lemon, Meaux mustard and a little green salad.

SPICED BEEF PANCAKES

To serve 6

1lb/450grms minced beef
4oz/100grms onion
1 tablespoon of vegetable oil
½ teaspoonful of dried mixed herbs
½ teaspoonful of cumin seeds
a clove of garlic
1oz/25grms plain flour
14oz/400grms tin of tomatoes
1 dessertspoonful of tomato pureé
6 shakes of tabasco

6 shakes of Worcestershire sauce
¼pt/150 ml brown stock
salt

6 pancakes, see page 93

1pt/600ml Bechamel sauce,
see page 87
6oz/175grms gruyere cheese
grated parmesan

Preparation
Chop the onion. Crush the garlic with a little salt. Drain and chop the tinned tomatoes, retaining the juice. Grate the gruyere.

Method
We commence by frying the onions in the vegetable oil with the mixed herbs, cumin seed, garlic and salt until golden brown. Then tip in the flour and the beef and cook for a few minutes until the meat is lightly browned. Now stir in the tomato pureé, tinned tomatoes, stock and as much tabasco and Worcestershire sauce as you like your pancakes spicy. Bring sharply to the boil, stirring all the time.

Cover and leave to simmer for 20 minutes.

Assembly
Light the grill. Warm through the Bechamel sauce. All that remains is to divide the spiced beef equally and fill the six pancakes before laying them in a shallow ovenproof dish and pouring over the Bechamel sauce. Sprinkle over the gruyere and parmesan. Put under the grill until golden brown and serve immediately with hot French or garlic bread.

MAIN COURSES

FEUILLETAGE of LOBSTER

Fresh lobster baked in a cream and white wine sauce inside individual parcels of puff pastry, accompanied by Hollandaise Sauce.

To serve 6

A 3lb/1½kilo lobster to yield
1lb/450grms lobster meat
12oz/350grms puff pastry
2oz/50grms butter
2oz/50grms block roux,
see page 95
6fl oz/150ml dry white wine
¼pt/150ml fish stock
¼pt/150ml double cream
a measure of brandy
the juice of ½ a lemon

a small clove of garlic
a pinch of mixed dried herbs
¼ teaspoonful of sugar
a shake of tabasco
salt and freshly ground
black pepper
1 egg
½ cup of milk
½pt/300ml Hollandaise sauce,
see page 90

Preparation
Make the egg wash by beating the egg in to the milk.
Crush the garlic with a little salt.
Put a large saucepan of salted water on to boil.

Method
As one is unable to tell visually when a lobster is fully cooked it is necessary to time how long it is in the water. Thus the 3lb lobster quoted in the ingredients above needs 45 minutes from the time the water boils. Anything larger will need an hour and something as small as 1lb would only need 20 minutes.

Lift the lobster from the water and allow to cool. Remove all the meat and chop in to chunks setting aside any coral (the streak of bright red eggs). Put a heavy saute pan on the heat with the butter. Finely chop the coral before tossing this in to the melted butter with the garlic and herbs. Flambé with the brandy and then pour in the white wine, fish stock, lemon juice, tabasco, sugar and seasoning. Bring sharply to the boil and whisk in the grated roux until the sauce becomes thick and smooth.

Remove from the heat and fold in the lobster meat first followed by the cream. Adjust the seasoning. It is now necessary to allow the whole mixture to cool completely and for this reason it is not a bad idea to make it the day before you wish to use it.

Preparation for assembling the feuilletages
Set the oven to No. 8/450 degrees.
Grease two baking trays.
Make up the Hollandaise sauce and keep warm.

We now come to the business of actually making and assembling the feuilletages.

We start by cutting the pastry in to six equal pieces which we roll in to rectangles 6in. x 8 in. Divide the chilled lobster mixture in to six equal parts and dollop them in to the centre of each piece of pastry leaving a broad border which should be brushed with egg wash.

Now we are ready to make the parcels and this is best achieved by first folding the two short sides over the top of the mixture, allowing a generous overlap. The ends should be crimped together. Remember that once the feuilletages are put in the oven the sauce will become liquid again and it is therefore vital that they are well sealed and free of any holes.

Arrange the six parcels on the baking trays leaving as much space as possible between them. Brush their surfaces with egg wash and put on the top shelf of the oven to bake for 10-15 minutes until golden brown.

Serve accompanied by the Hollandaise sauce.

FILLET of HALIBUT with BANANAS and MANGO CHUTNEY

To serve 4

4x6oz/175grms halibut steaks cut from a large fillet
with the skin removed
2 bananas
2 large tomatoes
4 dessertspoonfuls of mango chutney
4oz/100grms butter
the juice of 2 lemons
1oz/25 grms clarified butter, see page 96
1 tablespoonful of olive oil
1 tablespoonful of seasoned flour
parsley

Preparation

Peel the tomatoes. This is most easily done by briefly immersing them in boiling water until the skins start to split and peel off. Now chop them.
Peel and slice the bananas.
Roughly chop the chutney.
Combine all these with the lemon juice.
Preheat the oven to No.6/400 degrees.

Method

Dip the steaks in to the seasoned flour and pat off the excess.

Take a heavy sauté pan and heat the clarified butter and oil. Fry the steaks on both sides for a few minutes to seal them before transferring them to the oven dish. Spoon the banana mixture over the top of each steak and top it with a 1oz. knob of butter.

Place in the top of the oven and bake for 10-15 minutes. Serve decorated with parsley.

PAUPIETTE of SALMON STUFFED with MOUSSELINE

Salmon in salmon – the texture of the mousseline contrasting with a slice of the fish baked in a creamy wine sauce.

To serve 6

1lb 12oz/675grms fresh Scotch salmon fillet – tail end
$\frac{1}{2}$pt/300ml double cream
2 egg whites
salt and white pepper
grated nutmeg
1pt/600ml Bechamel sauce, see page 87
$\frac{1}{2}$pt/300ml double cream
$\frac{1}{4}$pt/150ml dry white wine
4oz/100grms puff pastry

Equipment A shallow ovenproof dish.

Preparation
Skin the salmon and remove any small bones.

Method
Our aim is to use part of the salmon for mousseline and part for slices to wrap it in. Start by cutting six horizontal slices of approximately 3oz each. Chop the remaining salmon in to chunks and liquidise with the nutmeg, salt and pepper. Add the egg whites. Liquidise again and finally add the double cream and give a long enough burst of the liquidiser to create a smooth creamy consistency. Transfer to a bowl and allow to stand in the fridge for at least 3hrs. to give sufficient time for the mousseline to become firm.

Preheat the oven to No.4/350 degrees. Divide the mousseline mixture in to six equal parts and roll up in the six slices of raw salmon. Place seam downwards in the ovenproof dish.

Turning our attention to the sauce, this is simply made by heating the Bechamel and wine together. Finish by stirring in the cream. Pour this over the waiting paupiettes and bake in the middle of the oven for 30 minutes testing that they are fully cooked – they should be firm to the touch.

While these are baking you have an opportunity to roll out the pastry and cut out crescents. Place them on a greased baking tray ready to be popped in to the oven for 10 minutes once the paupiettes are cooked and being kept warm. It will be necessary to increase the heat for this to No. 8/450 degrees.

Finally serve the paupiettes decorated with the crescents and some parsley.

ROAST JOHN DORY with FRESH HERB BUTTER

John Dory is one of nature's uglier fish and not that easy to find in the shops. It is however every bit as delicious as Turbot when plainly roasted and can be considerably cheaper.

To serve 4

A 5lb/2.25kilo John Dory
4oz/100grms butter
the juice of $\frac{1}{2}$ a lemon
a tablespoonful of freshly chopped herbs
(parsley, thyme, rosemary, tarragon)
olive oil
seasoned flour
freshly ground black pepper

Preparation
Preheat the over to No.7/425 degrees.
Oil a shallow ovenproof dish or roasting tin.

Method
Depending on your relationship with your fishmonger you may be able to persuade him to cut the available fish from one John Dory in to four good-sized steaks. If you are obliged to do it yourself, cut off the head and the guts that lie between the head and the underside of the fish. Also chop off the tail and the fins. This leaves a piece of fish approximately the shape of Africa which can be cut through the bone in to four pieces.

Dip each piece in to the seasoned flour. Pat off the excess and arrange, dark skin upwards, in the oiled dish. Brush all over with olive oil and bake for 15 minutes in the top of the oven. Remove from the oven and peel off the dark skin.

Spread the butter, herbs and lemon juice over the top of the fish and return to the top of the oven just long enough to melt the butter.

Serve immediately with new potatoes and a plain green vegetable.

TURBOT and MUSSEL PIE

An elegant fish pie.

To serve 4

4pts/2.4litres fresh mussels
1lb/450grms turbot fillet
2oz/50grms chopped onion
1pt/600ml Bechamel sauce, see page 8 7
½pt/300ml double cream
¼pt/150ml dry white wine
8oz/225grms puff pastry
1 egg
½ cup of milk
a pinch of ground white pepper

Equipment 4 round shallow pie dishes – the 7in. diameter earthenware gratin dishes from Elizabeth David are ideal.
A large covered saucepan.

Preparation
Beat the egg in to the milk to make the egg wash.
Clean the mussels by rinsing under plenty of cold water.
Remove the beards and discard any with open or damaged shells.
Skin the turbot fillet.
Preheat the oven to No. 5/375 degrees.

Method
Steam the mussels in the large covered pan with the wine, onion and pepper. Cook for approximately 15 minutes, shaking occasionally until all the shells have opened. Drain the mussels discarding any that have not opened. Reserve and strain the stock. Remove the mussels from their shells.

Boil the stock until it has reduced to ¼pt/150ml. Whisk in the Bechamel and then the cream. Bring to the boil and remove from the heat.

All that remains is to cut the turbot in to four equal parts and place one in the centre of each pie dish. Distribute the mussels and just cover with the sauce.

Roll out the pastry as thinly as possible to the shape of the pie dishes with ½in. overlap to allow the crust to be pulled over the edge of the pie dish and pressed to the side using a little water to help adhesion. Brush the surface with egg wash immediately and bake for 20 minutes in the middle of the oven until the pastry is golden brown.

This is delicious eaten straight from the dish.

BARBECUED CHICKEN BREAST

To serve 4

4 Chicken breasts complete with skin and bones
8 dried prunes
8 rashers of smoked back bacon
8 whole almonds – skinned
8x3in. sprigs of fresh rosemary
vegetable oil
salt and freshly ground black pepper

Equipment   A barbecue
A long skewer

Preparation
Soak the prunes overnight in cold tea.
Toast the almonds until golden in a low oven.
Stone the prunes and replace the stones with an almond.
Wrap a rasher of bacon round each prune and thread on to the oiled skewer.
Make the devils on horseback by wrapping the rashers of bacon around the
prunes and secure with a cocktail stick.

Method
Light the barbecue and allow to reach full heat. Liberally brush the chicken
breasts with oil and seal each side for a couple of minutes before seasoning
fairly generously. Push the sprigs of fresh rosemary under the breasts so that
they burn and scorch the meat.

Depending on the heat of the barbecue it will take 15-20 minutes for the
breasts to cook fully and it should be only in the last few minutes that the devils
on horseback are put over the coals, turning once.

Serve with baked potatoes, sour cream and chives.

CHICKEN BREAST STUFFED with PRAWNS and CREAM CHEESE

This is outstandingly the most popular chicken dish with our customers as chicken and prawns are marvellous bedfellows and taste exceptional when served crisp with Choron sauce.

To serve 6

6 Chicken breasts (skinned with just the wing bone remaining)
12oz/350grms peeled prawns
8oz/225grms cream cheese
4oz/100grms butter
freshly ground black pepper
a tablespoonful of chopped parsley
1 egg
$\frac{1}{2}$ cup of milk
8oz/225grms breadcrumbs, see page 93
1pt/600ml Choron sauce, see page 89
vegetable oil

Preparation
Preheat the oven to No. 7/425 degrees.
Oil a baking sheet.
In a shallow dish beat the egg in to the milk for the egg wash.
Drain the prawns.
Beat the cream cheese with the parsley and black pepper until it becomes soft before combining it with the prawns. This is the stuffing.
The chicken breasts must be placed on a wooden board with the insides uppermost to reveal a small flap of meat that should be laid back. Lightly beat both the breast and the flap with a rolling pin.
Now divide the prawn and cream cheese mixture in to 6 equal parts and position on the breasts in such a way that the flap can be brought over to cover. Lift the breasts off the board, turn them over, tucking the edges underneath to recreate the original shape.
Flour, egg wash and breadcrumb before placing on a baking tray with a knob of butter ready for roasting.

Method
Roast in the top of the oven for 15-20 minutes until golden. Serve with plenty of Choron sauce.

CROUSTADE of CHICKEN BREAST with QUAILS EGGS

Breast of Chicken in an open tart with Hollandaise sauce.

To serve 4

4 Chicken breasts (skinned with just the wing bone remaining)
8oz/335grms shortcrust pastry, see page 92
½ quantity of duxelle stuffing, see page 94
12 quails eggs
½pt/300ml Hollandaise sauce, see page 90
4fl oz/100ml dry white wine
2oz/50grms butter
vegetable oil
salt and freshly ground black pepper

Equipment 4 x barquette or similar oval moulds about 5in. long and 2½in. to 3in. wide.

Preparation
Preheat the oven to No. 6/400 degrees
Lightly oil the barquette moulds
Roll out the pastry, line the moulds, prick all over and bake blind.
Boil the quails eggs for 2-3 minutes. Refresh under cold water and peel carefully.
Make the duxelle stuffing and keep it warm.
Make the Hollandaise sauce and stand it in a warm place.

Method
Commence by poaching the chicken breasts in a covered pan with the butter and wine. Season. This should take about 10-12 minutes at which point the peeled quails eggs can be dropped in to the liquor to warm them up.

The next move is to spread an even layer of duxelle across the bases of the four croustades and set a chicken breast in the middle of each. Surround with 3 quails eggs and slip in to the oven to keep warm while you reduce the remaining white wine liquor in an uncovered pan to approximately 2fl oz/50ml. Take off the heat and whisk in the Hollandaise and pour over the top of the waiting croustades.

Serve immediately with a little parsley.

PHEASANT TART

One of our favourite ways of serving Pheasant.

To serve 4

8oz/225grms shortcrust pastry,
see page 92
2 medium pheasants – about
1½lbs/675grms each
1pt/600ml Bechamel sauce,
see page 8 7
6oz/175grms mushrooms

5fl oz/150ml dry white wine
a measure of brandy
¼pt/50ml double cream
the juice of ¼ of a lemon
salt and freshly ground
black pepper

Equipment   4 flan tins – 4in. diameter x ¾in. deep.

Preparation
Preheat the oven to No. 5/375 degrees. Line the pastry cases with the pastry, prick all over with a fork and bake blind until crisp and golden. Make the Bechamel sauce and set aside. Wipe and slice the mushrooms.

Method
Firstly the pheasants should be roasted. We are not going to use the legs so remove these and set aside for another dish. Smear the breasts with butter and put in a roasting tray in the middle of the oven for 20-30 minutes until just cooked. Remove them after they are done and keep warm.

It is a nice idea to use a little of the pheasant fat from the roasting tray in which to fry the sliced mushrooms. Other than that the rest of this fat should be poured off leaving only the tasty sediment and meat juices. It is in to these that the white wine should be stirred.

Flambé the mushrooms with the brandy while you are frying them and then pour over the wine mixture from the roasting tin.

All that remains is to heat up the Bechamel sauce, stir in the mushrooms, double cream and lemon juice and adjust the seasoning before assembling the complete dish.

Assembly
This should be left until the moment before eating and should be done as follows: Cut the breasts off the carcass and carve in to thickish slices. Arrange the meat in the waiting tart cases and pour over the creamy mushroom sauce.

ROAST DUCKLING with ORANGE and BRANDY SAUCE

To serve 4

THE DUCK
2x3½lb/1.5 kilo fresh ducks – oven ready
salt

ORANGE AND BRANDY SAUCE
2 oranges
4fl oz/100ml brandy
1 tablespoonful of redcurrant jelly
2 tablespoonfuls of Worcestershire sauce
1 teaspoonful of prepared English mustard
1pt/600ml Brown sauce, see page 88
1 lemon

Preparation
Preheat the oven to No. 7/425 degrees. Prick the duck well all over and rub with salt. Pare the zest from the oranges and cut into thin strips. Squeeze the juice from the oranges and the lemon.

Method
Roast the ducks upside down, one inch apart in the middle of the oven for 1½hrs. After this time take them out and allow to cool for 30 minutes. The birds will then be sufficiently cool to remove the breast and legs from the carcasses and these should be returned to the oven for 20 minutes in a fresh tray, skin side upwards to finish cooking and go crisp.

To make the fresh orange sauce take a sauté pan and flambé all the zest with the brandy before stirring in the orange and lemon juice, Worcestershire sauce, redcurrant jelly and English mustard. Now pour the Brown sauce and heat through stirring all the time.

Accompany the duck with an orange and watercress salad and hand the sauce separately.

ROAST DUCKLING with PEASE PUDDING and SPRING ONION SAUCE

To serve 4

THE DUCK
2x3½lb/1.5 kilos fresh ducks –
oven ready
½ teaspoonful of dried sage
1 tablespoonful of vegetable oil
salt and freshly ground
black pepper

SPRING ONION SAUCE
1 large bunch of spring onions
2oz/50grms butter
1oz/25grms plain flour

¾pt/450ml milk
¼ chicken stock cube
a bay leaf
salt and freshly ground
black pepper

PEASE PUDDING
8oz/225grms yellow split peas
1pt/600ml water
1 small onion
salt and freshly ground
black pepper

Preparation the day before
This is not absolutely necessary but if you wish to shorten the cooking time for the pease pudding you may soak the split peas in tepid water overnight.

Preparation the following day
Make a paste with the sage, oil, half a teaspoonful of salt and half a teaspoonful of black pepper.
Prick the ducks all over and rub this paste in to the flesh inside and out.
Trim the spring onions leaving a fair amount of green and cut them in to one inch lengths.
Peel and chop the onion for the pease pudding.
Preheat the oven to No. 7/425 degrees.

Method
Bring the split peas slowly to the boil in the water with the onion, salt and black pepper. Cover and leave to simmer until soft. This will take approximately 1hr. if you are using soaked peas or about 1½hrs. and ½pt/300ml extra water if you have not had time to soak them overnight. Keep an eye on the water level in case you are running dry. Conversely drain off any excess water at the end.

At the end of this time stir with a wooden spoon to the consistency of a thick pea soup and pour in to an earthenware dish.

Once the pease pudding is simmering as described above you will have time to tackle the ducks. They should be roasted upside down one inch apart in the middle of the oven for $1\frac{1}{2}$hrs. after which they may be taken out and allowed to cool for 30 minutes. At the end of this time the birds will be sufficiently cool to remove the breast and legs from the carcasses and these should be returned to the oven for 20 minutes in a fresh tray, skin side upwards to finish cooking and go crisp.

The pease pudding now in its earthenware dish should also go in to the oven at the same time having first been sprinkled with some of the duck dripping.

Finally while these two are cooking make the Spring Onion Sauce by melting the butter in a saucepan and frying the onions until soft. Stir in the flour and cook for a few moments before gradually introducing the milk. Bring to the boil, stirring all the time. Crumble in the stock cube adjust the seasoning and leave for 5 minutes over a low heat. Transfer to a warm jug and keep hot.

To serve
Position the duck on a bed of the pease pudding and hand the onion sauce separately.

STEAK and PIGEON PIE

To serve 4

1lb 8oz/675grms
Chuck Steak
3 pigeons
8oz/200grms onion
4oz/100grms button mushrooms
1pt/600ml strong beer
1pt/600ml water
1 heaped tablespoonful of
tomato pureé
1 dessertspoonful of
Worcestershire sauce
$\frac{1}{2}$ teaspoonful of dried or

Fresh mixed herbs
2 bay leaves
1 tablespoonful of
vegetable oil
2oz/50grms block roux,
see page 95
salt and freshly ground
black pepper
1 egg
$\frac{1}{2}$ cup of milk
8oz/225grms hazelnut pastry,
see page 92

Equipment A $2\frac{1}{2}$pt/1.5 litre pie dish
A pie bird – or china egg cup

Preparation

Chop the onion. Grate the roux. Beat the egg in to the milk to make the egg wash. Cut the steak in to 1in. pieces, trimming off any excess fat. Wipe and quarter the mushrooms.

The main meat on a pigeon is of course the breasts and these should be removed with a sharp knife together with any small pieces of meat that you are able to slice off the legs. As much of the flavour of a pigeon's carcass is to be found around its backbone (it is here that most of the blood vessels run) this should be cut away from the rest and placed on one side. Discard the residue.

Method

Take a heavy based sauté pan and cook the onions, mushrooms, bay leaves, herbs, salt and pepper in the vegetable oil until soft. Add the pigeons, steak and the backbones and cook to seal over a brisk flame for up to 5 minutes.

Now we can add the tomato pureé, water, beer and Worcestershire sauce and bring to the boil before allowing to simmer under cover for 2-2$\frac{1}{2}$hrs. until the steak is tender.

Lift out the backbones and discard. Turn up the flame and remove the cover to reduce the liquor to approximately 1 pint. Thicken by stirring in the grated roux and at this stage adjust the seasoning and make any alteration to the colour that you like using gravy browning.

In an ideal world one would allow the mixture to cool and stand overnight in the fridge to allow the full flavours to develop.

The pie is simply made, as one might expect, by transferring the mixture in to a dish complete with pie bird in the middle. Wet the edges and cover with pastry. Brush with egg wash and bake in a No. 5/375 degrees oven for $\frac{3}{4}$-1hr. until the pastry is golden.

TURKEY STEAK with AVOCADO and SMOKED SALMON

To serve 4

4x8oz/225grms turkey steaks cut thickly from the breast
1 avocado – slightly underripe
4 slices of smoked salmon – about 1oz/25grms each
½pt/300ml Choron sauce, see page 89
vegetable oil
freshly ground black pepper

Preparation
Make the Choron sauce and keep it warm.
Put the smoked salmon in a warm part of the kitchen.
Peel and slice the avocado
Light the grill.

Method
Fry the turkey steaks in the oil for between 6-8 minutes each side until golden and firm to the touch. Transfer to the grill pan and arrange the slices of avocado on the top, grind a little black pepper, brush lightly with oil and put under the grill for 2-3 minutes to warm the avocado through.

Finally place the steaks on a plate, lay a slice of smoked salmon over the top and pour a generous amount of Choron sauce over that. Serve immediately.

VENISON BOURGUIGNONNE

To serve 4

2lbs/1 kilo Shoulder of Venison
6oz/175grms small
button mushrooms
8 button onions
4 rashers of unsmoked
streaky bacon
1pt/600ml Brown stock
1pt/600ml red wine
1oz/25grms good dripping

2oz/50grms plain flour
1 heaped tablespoonful of
tomato pureé
a clove of garlic
3 bay leaves
a bunch of fresh herbs
salt and freshly ground
black pepper

Equipment   A large casserole

Preparation the day before
Crush the garlic with a little salt. Cut the venison in to 1in. pieces trimming off
any excess fat and sinew. Tie the herbs in a bunch. Marinate the venison
overnight in the wine with the garlic, pepper, salt, herbs and bay leaves.

Preparation the following day
Preheat the oven to No. 5/375 degrees. Peel the onions. Cut the bacon in to
1in. pieces. Wipe the mushrooms. Drain the marinade from the meat and
reserve.

Method
Take a heavy based sauté pan and melt the dripping. Seal the venison over a
strong flame a few pieces at a time, putting them in to the casserole once
browned.

Next fry the mushrooms, bacon and onions until they too are just golden.
Sprinkle in the flour and stir to make a roux with the remaining dripping (add
extra dripping if necessary). Cook for a few minutes and then pour in the tomato
pureé, brown stock and marinade – including the bunch of herbs and bay
leaves.

Bring to the boil, stirring continuously and pour over the waiting venison. Cover
the casserole and put in the middle of the oven for 2 hrs.

Remove the herbs, correct the seasoning and serve with crisply fried croutes or
even Yorkshire pudding.

This dish will improve in flavour if allowed to stand overnight in the fridge.

CROUSTADE of FILLET STEAK and GRUYERE

A fillet steak baked with a field mushroom and gruyere cheese on puff pastry.

To serve 4

4x6oz-80z/175-225grms tournedos fillet steaks – trimmed
4 large field or flat mushrooms roughly the same size as the steaks
4x2oz/50grms slices of gruyere cheese
8oz/225grms puff pastry
vegetable oil
salt and fresh ground black pepper

Preparation
Preheat the oven to No. 8/450 degrees.
Wipe the mushrooms and remove the stalks.

Method
Commence by sealing the steaks in hot oil a few seconds each side, followed by the mushrooms which should be cooked until soft. Set aside and allow to cool.

The next task is to roll out the pastry to the broad shape of the steaks, allowing a border of at least $1\frac{1}{2}$in. Place on a baking tray and position the fillet steaks in the centre of each croustade. Season and top with a mushroom, followed by a slice of gruyere cheese.

Bake in the top of the oven for 10-15 minutes by which time the cheese will have melted and the steak itself will be nicely rare. The $1\frac{1}{2}$in. border of puff pastry will rise around the steak and serve to contain the juices and melted cheese.

If you prefer the steaks better done it is wise to seal them for longer at the beginning rather than baking them for longer now.

Serve at once.

KEBAB of FILLET STEAK and SCALLOPS

People tend to be surprised at this combination – however the soft texture and delicate flavour of fresh scallops and fillet steak go beautifully together especially when accompanied by Bearnaise Sauce.

To serve 4

1lb 4oz/550grms trimmed fillet steak
12 large scallops
12 large button mushrooms
4 rashers of smoked back bacon
12 small bay leaves
salt and freshly ground black pepper
vegetable oil
1 cup of rice – cooked plain
½pt/300ml Bearnaise sauce, see page 86

Equipment 4 x 12in. skewers.

Preparation
Cut the steak in to 16 evenly-sized pieces.
Clean the scallops and remove the intestines.
Wipe the mushrooms and remove the stalks.
Cut each rasher of bacon in to 3 pieces.
Make the Bearnaise sauce and keep warm.
Prepare the rice.

Method
Before any ingredients can be put on the skewers we must first seal the fillet steak and the scallops in separate pans by cooking them in hot oil a few at a time. Cook the mushrooms in oil until they are soft. Light the grill.

Now arrange the ingredients on the skewers in the following order: fillet steak, bacon, mushroom, scallop, bay leaf, ending with fillet steak. Season and put under the grill, turning once.

If you cook the kebab so that the fillet steak is nicely pink in the middle all the other ingredients will be cooked just right. Serve on the rice with Bearnaise Sauce.

LES TROIS FILETS

Three different meats, all served together but each with a separate accompaniment.

To serve 4

4x2-3oz/50-75grms tournedos fillet steaks
12oz/350grms pork fillet (tenderloin)
12oz/350grms lamb fillet from either the middle neck or best end.
4 large flat mushrooms
vegetable oil
salt and freshly ground black pepper
½pt/300ml Barbecue sauce, see page 85
½pt/300ml Hollandaise sauce, see page 90

Preparation
Light the grill
Trim the meat of all fat and sinew
Cut the pork and lamb fillet in to 3oz steaks
Wipe the mushrooms and remove the stalks
Make the Barbecue sauce and the Hollandaise sauce and keep warm.

Method
Everything can be cooked in the same frying pan providing that the timing is organised so that the pork which needs the longest cooking goes in first, followed after a few minutes by the lamb and mushrooms and finally, depending on how you like them cooked, the fillet steaks.

Season as required and serve by accompanying the fillet steak with a little Hollandaise, the pork with Barbecue sauce and the lamb on a mushroom.

ROAST SIRLOIN of BEEF with CHESTNUT, CREAM and SHERRY SAUCE

To serve 4

2lb/1 kilo best Scotch sirloin – trimmed
$\frac{1}{2}$pt/300ml Bechamel sauce, see page 87
$\frac{1}{4}$pt/150ml double cream
8oz/225grms whole peeled chestnuts
4fl oz/100ml dry sherry
the juice of $\frac{1}{4}$ of a lemon
$\frac{1}{4}$ teaspoonful of French mustard
$\frac{1}{2}$ teaspoonful of freshly chopped tarragon
olive oil
salt and freshly ground black pepper

Preparation
Preheat the oven to No. 6/400 degrees.

Method
Firstly to roast the sirloin brush it with oil and season generously with salt and black pepper before putting it in to the oven for 15 minutes per pound.

Once roasted, lift the joint out of the roasting tray and allow to stand in a warm place for 15 minutes.

We want to make the sauce with the juices from the beef which means that we must first pour off the fat. Combine the juices that remain in the tray with the sherry, lemon juice, mustard and tarragon. Bring to the boil and then whisk in the Bechamel sauce. Bring to the boil again before finally stirring in the cream and peeled chestnuts. Heat through and adjust the seasoning.

Transfer to a sauce boat and keep hot while you carve the beef in to thick rare slices decorated with watercress.

Hand the sauce separately.

SIRLOIN STEAK with BUTTERED SQUID

To serve 4

4x8oz/225grms thick Scotch sirloin steaks – trimmed
1lb/450grms fresh squid
4oz/100grms butter
the juice of a lemon
vegetable oil
grated nutmeg
salt and freshly ground black pepper

Preparation
Prepare the squid as in the recipe for Squid Stew on page **26**
Light the grill.

Method
Firstly the steaks should be sealed on both sides in hot oil for a few seconds in a heavy frying pan, before being seasoned and transferred to the preheated grill where they should continue to be cooked to your taste.

The frying pan should be drained and the butter tipped in and melted ready for the squid which needs to be cooked over medium heat until just opaque when the lemon juice and nutmeg is also stirred in. Allow the butter and lemon juice to boil for a moment or two to produce a sauce-like consistency. Remove the pan from the heat.

By now the steaks under the grill should be ready and all that remains is to tip the squid mixture in equal parts over them and serve immediately.

RACK of LAMB with APRICOT SAUCE

This is our favourite way of cooking lamb at The Hungry Monk and demands the quality of home-produced rather than imported lamb.

To serve 2

1 best end of English lamb (Ask your butcher to remove the chine *without* cutting in to the eye of the meat and to trim the rib bones to a uniform length.)
4oz/100grms breadcrumbs, see page 93
1 tablespoonful of plain flour
1 egg
½ a cup of milk
4 fresh apricots
3oz/75grms granulated sugar
olive oil
½pt/300ml Brown sauce, see page 88
1 tablespoonful of Worcestershire sauce
1 level teaspoonful of Dijon mustard
3fl oz/75ml red wine
the juice of ½ a lemon

Preparation
Preheat the oven to No. 6/400 degrees.
Beat the egg in to the milk to make the egg wash.

The ideal look for roast rack of lamb is for the ribs to be exposed and nearly all the fat, together with the tip of the blade bone, removed. To heighten the effect trim away the meat and fat between each rib for approximately 1½in. from the end. Dip the rack in to the flour, brush with egg wash and liberally coat with breadcrumbs. leaving the ribs uncovered. Halve and stone the apricots.

Method
Put the lamb in to a roasting tin, dribble a little oil over the top and place in the middle of the oven. Whilst this is roasting we can make the sauce.

Start by poaching the apricots with the sugar in sufficient water to cover until just soft. Now take a separate pan and cook together the brown sauce, Worcestershire sauce, lemon juice, red wine, Dijon mustard and two tablespoonfuls of the apricot liquor. Bring to the boil. Drain the apricots and tip them in to the sauce. Keep warm.

When the lamb is cooked transfer to a carving board and either cut in half or in to chops.

Hand the sauce separately.

ROAST LOIN of LAMB with PARSLEY and LEMON BUTTER

To serve 6

THE LAMB
2x2½lb/just over 1 kilo loins of
English lamb (ask your butcher to
bone them)
1oz/25grms plain flour
¾pt/450ml brown stock
5fl oz/125ml red wine
a few drops of soy sauce
salt and freshly ground
black pepper

PARSLEY BUTTER
8oz/225grms butter
2 heaped tablespoonfuls of finely
chopped parsley
the juice of ½ a lemon
freshly ground black pepper

Preparation
Preheat the oven to No. 6/400 degrees.
Now for a bit of butchery! You can ask your butcher to roll the loins for you but
the chances are he will leave in too much fat – it is therefore better to do it
yourself.
There is fat on both sides of the loin and as much of this as possible should be
sliced away with a very sharp knife so that you are left with the eye of the meat
attached to a rectangular flap of meat and fat, and separately the fillet. The fillet
should be laid alongside the eye once you have finished trimming and the
middle of the joint be seasoned with salt and black pepper. Roll up tightly and
tie with string round each end and the middle. Sprinkle with salt and place the
joints one inch apart in a roasting tin.

The Parsley Butter
Chop the butter in to a bowl with the parsley, lemon juice and black pepper.
Knead together with your hand. Return the mixture to the original butter
wrapper and roll up in to a cylinder. Refrigerate.

Method
The loins should be roasted in the top half of the oven for between 35 and 45
minutes depending on how pink you like your meat. Once they are cooked lift
them out of the tray and keep warm. We shall make the gravy in the roasting
tray and must therefore start by pouring off the surface fat before putting the
tray over a low flame. Sprinkle in the flour and stir thoroughly, scraping the
goodness from the sides of the tin. Tip in the red wine and stock and bring
sharply to the boil, stirring all the time. Shake in a few drops of soy sauce to
enrich the colour and flavour. Transfer to a warm jug.

Turning our attention to the parsley and lemon butter, this will now be well refrigerated and can therefore be cut in to slices.

All that remains is to carve the loins in to thick slices topped with the parsley and lemon butter and accompanied by the gravy.

This is a clear case for going to the extra trouble of making some dauphinoise potatoes and decorating with watercress.

MEDALLIONS of PORK FILLET with AVOCADO, CREAM and CURRY SAUCE,

This is a particularly good dish as the sauce is not hot but has a wonderfully deep flavour that is quite excellent with pork.

To serve 4

1lb 8oz/675grms trimmed port fillet (tenderloin)
1 avocado – slightly underripe
4oz/100grms onion
2oz/50grms celery
2oz/50grms cooking apple
1 clove of garlic
1 tablespoonful of flaked almonds
1 dessertspoonful of sultanas
vegetable oil
the juice of $\frac{1}{2}$ a lemon
$\frac{3}{4}$pt/450ml Bechamel sauce, see page 87
5fl oz/125ml double cream
a teaspoonful of curry powder
a pinch of cumin seed
salt
1 cup of rice – cooked plain

Preparation
Crush the garlic with a little salt. Chop the onion and celery finely. Peel, core and grate the apple. Cut the pork in to $\frac{1}{2}$in. thick slices. Peel and slice the avocado. Prepare the rice.

Method
We need a heavy-based pan that is large enough to accommodate all the ingredients except the rice. Start by heating the oil together with the onion, celery, almonds, garlic, cumin seed and the salt. Cook until golden and then introduce the pork and sultanas. Continue over a brisk flame for 5 minutes keeping everything on the move.

Now we can stir in the curry powder, apple, lemon juice and Bechamel sauce and bring everything to the boil. Simmer for 5 minutes before adding the cream and avocado.

Heat through and serve immediately with rice.

NOISETTES of PORK with TEQUILA and PEPPERCORN SAUCE

To serve 4

8 thick slices of boned loin of pork with the excess fat trimmed off.
1oz/25grms clarified butter, see page 96
1 clove of garlic
1 tablespoonful of pink peppercorns and some of their juice
½pt/300ml Bechamel sauce, see page 87
3fl oz/75ml dry sherry
2fl oz/50ml tequila
7fl oz/175ml double cream
salt

Preparation
Light the grill. Crush the garlic with a little salt.

Method
First the pork which should be sealed on both sides for a few seconds in the hot clarified butter. Lift out and transfer to the grill where the cooking can continue whilst the sauce is made.

Tip the garlic in to the remains of the hot butter and fry until golden, then flambé with the tequila. Follow this by pouring in the sherry, Bechamel sauce, peppercorns with their juice and salt. Bring to the boil and stir in the cream and heat through.

If all is going to plan the noisettes of pork should now be ready and can be arranged on the plates with watercress. Pour over the tequila sauce and serve immediately.

AUBERGINE and LENTIL PANCAKE

To serve 6

THE PANCAKE
8oz/225grms red or brown lentils
8oz/225grms onion
1lb 8oz/675grms aubergines
1pt/600ml water or vegetable
stock
6fl oz/150ml vegetable oil
the juice of a lemon
2 medium cloves of garlic
a good pinch of cumin seed
salt and freshly ground
black pepper
12 pancakes, see page 93
parmesan cheese

CHEESE SAUCE
1pt/600ml Bechamel sauce,
see page 87
2 tablespoonfuls of
double cream
3oz/75grms good Cheddar
$\frac{1}{2}$ teaspoonful of prepared English
mustard

Preparation the day before
This is not absolutely necessary but it you wish to shorten the cooking time for
this dish you may soak the lentils in tepid water overnight.

Preparation the following day
Slice the aubergines, sprinkle with salt and leave covered for at least 30
minutes. This draws out the bitter, indigestible juices. Rinse under cold water
and pat dry with a towel.
Chop the onion.
Crush the garlic with a little salt.
Grate the Cheddar.
Make the pancakes.

Method
The first task is to get the lentils on to cook. Bring them slowly to the boil in the
water or vegetable stock, cover and leave to simmer until soft. This will take
10-15 minutes if you are using soaked lentils, or about 45 minutes if you have
not had time to soak them overnight. Keep an eye on the water level in case
you are running dry. Conversely drain off any excess water at the end.

Whilst the lentils are cooking make the cheese sauce by heating the Bechamel
and stirring in the cheddar, followed by the mustard and cream. Set aside.

Next take a sauté pan and heat the oil. Tip in the garlic, onion, aubergines,
cumin seed and cook until soft. Then add the lemon juice and cooked lentils.

Pass the entire contents of this pan through a liquidiser and spread on the waiting pancakes after which they may be rolled up and arranged in a greased ovenproof dish.

Light the grill. Pour over the cheese sauce, sprinkle on the parmesan and put the whole lot under the grill until golden.

HOT VEGETABLE ROULADE

Vegetarians often complain that restaurants don't care about them. We have enjoyed developing special dishes such as this.

To serve 6

THE ROULADE
1lb/450grms frozen
leaf spinach
5 eggs
grated nutmeg
salt and freshly ground
black pepper

THE FILLING
1lb/450grms carrots
4oz/100grms onion
4oz/100grms celery

4oz/100grms green and red
peppers
4oz/100grms courgettes
4oz/100grms button mushrooms
12 peeled chestnuts
2 fresh tomatoes
a clove of garlic
a small bunch of fresh herbs
a tablespoonful of
vegetable oil
salt and freshly ground
black pepper

Equipment A shallow baking tray 16in. x 12 in. or two 8in. x 12in. if you have a small oven.

Preparation
Boil the spinach in salted water until cooked. Refresh under cold running water.
Drain and squeeze very dry in a tea towel.
Separate the eggs.
Cut a piece of greaseproof paper that is large enough to exactly cover the base and sides of the baking tray. As we need to oil both sides of this paper the best way is to oil the tray itself and then press first one side of the paper in to place, lift it off, turn it over and press the other side down.
Wipe and slice the mushrooms.
Peel and slice the carrots.
Finely chop the onion, celery, peppers and herbs.
Crush the garlic with a little salt.
Thinly slice the courgettes.
Skin the tomatoes by briefly immersing them in boiling water.
When the skin splits, peel it off and chop the flesh.
Preheat the oven to No. 8/450 degrees.

Method

THE ROULADE BASE

Liquidise the cooked spinach with the egg yolks, salt, pepper and nutmeg.

In a separate bowl whip the egg whites until they are stiff. Fold the spinach puree in to the egg whites and spread the mixture to an even thickness over the greaseproof paper. Bake in the top of the oven for 8-10 minutes until slightly risen, firm to the touch and colouring slightly. Allow to cool in the tray.

THE FILLING

Firstly the carrots must go to boil in some salted water.
In a heavy based sauté pan heat the oil and briefly cook the onion, celery, peppers, courgettes, mushrooms, garlic and herbs, keeping everything on the move. Tip in the tomatoes and continue to cook until all the excess juices have evaporated. Season and set aside.
Returning to the carrots which should be cooked by now, drain them and mash to a pureé.
All that remains is to tip the contents of the sauté pan together with the chestnuts in to the carrot purée and set the whole mixture on one side and keep warm while you go and do battle with the roulade base.
We are out to produce something that looks a bit like a Swiss roll. Start by removing the greaseproof paper from the base. This is best done by gently placing it face down on a fresh piece of paper and easing off the greaseproof, starting at the corners and side edges. Great care must be taken here as it is only too easy to tear the base which makes rolling up with a filling inside very difficult.

Assembly

The final task is to cover the base with the vegetable mixture – however because the whole thing is about to be rolled it makes life very much easier if you leave a one inch border clear at the beginning of the roll and again at the end.

Start with the uncovered border furthest away from you and gently roll the base up towards you using the greaseproof paper to give even support. Cut in thick slices. Arrange on a hot serving plate and if necessary flash back in to the hot oven.

CARROT and PARSNIP PUREE

This dish cannot be too highly recommended. It gives great elegance to two fairly cheap vegetables and has proved to be one of the all time favourites of the Hungry Monk.

1lb/450grms carrots – peeled and sliced
1lb/450grms parsnips – peeled and sliced
2oz/50grms butter
2 cloves of garlic crushed with a little salt
salt and freshly ground black pepper

Boil the vegetables until soft in salted water, drain and then mash together with the garlic, butter and black pepper until smooth.

DAUPHINOISE POTATOES

3lbs/1.5 kilos potatoes – peeled and finely sliced
$\frac{1}{2}$pt/300ml single cream
2oz/50grms butter
a clove of garlic crushed with a little salt
salt and freshly ground black pepper

Mix the cream, garlic, salt and black pepper in a bowl. Toss in the potatoes and coat thoroughly. Transfer to a buttered shallow ovenproof dish arranging the best slices in an overlapping pattern across the top. Brush with butter and bake in the middle of a No. 5/375 degrees oven for $1\frac{1}{2}$ hrs. until crisp and golden.

KOHL RABI BOULANGERE

Kohl Rabi is a less pungent but otherwise similar vegetable to turnip.

2lbs/1 kilo Kohl Rabi – peeled and sliced
8oz/225grms onion – finely sliced
1 small cooking apple – peeled and grated
3oz/75grms butter
$\frac{1}{4}$pt/150ml chicken stock
salt and freshly ground black pepper

Toss the kohl rabi, onion and apple together and tip in to a buttered ovenproof dish. Pour over the stock. Brush the top with butter and bake in a No. 4/350 degrees oven for 45 minutes – 1 hour until golden brown.

RED CABBAGE

2lb/1 kilo red cabbage – shredded
1 small cooking apple – peeled and grated
1 small onion – finely chopped
1 level teaspoonful of salt
1 level teaspoonful of sugar
2 tablespoonfuls of red wine vinegar
5fl oz/125ml red wine

Steam all the ingredients in a covered pan over a low flame for 45 minutes or bake in a No. 4/350 degrees oven for the same length of time. Finish with a knob of butter.

STIR-FRIED COURGETTES

2lbs/1 kilo courgettes – thinly sliced
2 tablespoonfuls of vegetable oil
1 teaspoonful of fresh chervil – chopped
salt and freshly ground black pepper

The essence of this is not to overcook the courgettes. Stir-fry with the vegetable oil, salt and black pepper over a high flame in a wok or something similar for 2-3 minutes. Sprinkle in the chervil just before serving.

PUDDINGS

CHOCOLATE FUDGE and ORANGE PIE

To serve 8-12

8oz/225grms shortcrust pastry, see page 92
1 tin of Banoffi Toffee,
(see Banoffi Ice Cream on page 82)
8oz/225grms Bournville plain chocolate
2oz/50grms cocoa powder
a tablespoonful of hot water
$\frac{1}{2}$pt/300ml double cream
a large measure of brandy
1oz/25grms castor sugar
the grated zest on an orange

Equipment A 10in. diameter x 1$\frac{1}{2}$in. deep flan dish.

Preparation
Preheat the oven to No. 6/400 degrees
Grease the flan dish and line with the pastry. Prick all over with a fork and bake blind until crisp and lightly coloured.
Grate 2oz/50grms of the plain chocolate.

Method
In a double saucepan break the remaining chocolate in to chunks and melt before stirring in the hot water. Combine this with the Banoffi Toffee and cocoa powder until you have a smooth consistency. This can now be spread across the base of the tart and allowed to cool completely.

Next the double cream must be whipped until stiff with the castor sugar, brandy and orange zest before this too is spread across the surface of the tart.

Finish by sprinkling the grated chocolate over the top.

CHOCOLATE MARQUISE

To serve 8-10

1lb/450grms best plain chocolate
1pt/600ml double cream
a wine glass of rum
1 packet of Langues de Chat biscuits

Equipment A loaf tin – 2pts/1.2 litres capacity

Preparation
Line the loaf tin with lightly oiled greaseproof paper. Briefly dip the biscuits in the rum and line the bottom and sides of the tin facing the rounded pale side inwards. Keep some in reserve for the top.

Method
In a double saucepan melt the chocolate. Take off the heat and stir in 6 tablespoonfuls of rum and the cream. Pour the mixture in to the waiting tin and finish by covering with the remaining rum soaked biscuits. Allow to set for 24 hrs. in the fridge and look forward to dazzling your friends with thickish slices of a very delicious pudding indeed.

Serve with thin coffee cream or whipped cream or even fresh raspberry pureé.

CHOCOLATE PRALINE SLICE

To serve 8-10

1lb 8oz/675grms plain Bournville chocolate
12oz/350grms praline, see page 96
6oz/150grms soaked raisins, see page 95
2oz/50grms unsalted butter
4fl oz/100ml water

Equipment A loaf or cake tin – 2pts/1.2 litres capacity

Preparation
Drain the raisins.

Method
Put a saucepan of water on to boil. Break the chocolate up in to pieces and combine with the water in the bowl over the pan of hot water until the chocolate is melted. Remove from the heat and stir to a smooth cream. Allow to cool to blood heat.

Beat in the butter a knob at a time before tipping in the raisins and praline. Stir thoroughly and spoon in to the tin. Refrigerate for 24hrs.

To turn out and serve, slide a knife around the edges of the tin and briefly dunk the base in a basin of hot water to loosen the bottom. Turn out to a serving plate and serve cut in to thin crisp slices with whipped cream.

HOT CHOCOLATE CAKE with ICE CREAM and CHOCOLATE SAUCE

To serve 6-8

THE CAKE
6oz/150grms butter
6oz/150grms castor sugar
3 eggs
4oz/100grms plain flour
2oz/50grms cocoa powder
1 level teaspoonful of
baking powder

THE SAUCE
1lb/450grms best plain chocolate
8fl oz/240 ml strong coffee

Equipment A cake tin 7in. diameter x 3in. deep.

Preparation
Preheat the oven to No. 3/325 degrees.
Grease the cake tin.
Sift together the flour, cocoa and baking powder.

Method
The cake is made in the usual way by beating the butter and sugar together until white, before stirring in the eggs and thoroughly folding in the flour, cocoa and baking powder.

Spoon the mixture in to the baking tin and bake in the middle of the oven for $1\frac{1}{4}$hrs. to $1\frac{1}{2}$hrs. until firm to the touch. Cool on a wire rack.

As this cake must be eaten warm, the ideal is to serve it straight away with ice cream and chocolate sauce. However this is not always possible in which case you can heat it up, wrapped in tin foil for 5-8 minutes in a hot oven or give it a quick burst, unwrapped, in a microwave.

Combine both ingredients in a bowl over a pan of hot water until the chocolate is melted. Stir to a smooth sauce and serve.

HOT MADEIRA CAKE with ICE CREAM and BUTTERSCOTCH SAUCE

To serve 6-8

THE CAKE
6oz/150grms butter
6oz/150grms castor sugar
3 eggs
6oz/150grms sifted self-raising
flour

THE SAUCE
1lb/450grms golden syrup
4oz/100grms butter

Equipment A cake tin 7in. diameter x 3in. deep.

Preparation
Preheat the oven to No. 3/325 degrees
Grease the cake tin

Method
The cake is made in the usual way by beating the butter and sugar together until white before stirring in the eggs and thoroughly folding in the flour.

Spoon the mixture in to the baking tin and bake in the middle of the oven for $1\frac{1}{4}$hrs. to $1\frac{1}{2}$hrs. until firm to the touch. Cool on a wire rack.

As this cake must be eaten warm, the ideal is to serve it straight away with ice cream and butterscotch sauce. However this is not alway possible in which case you can heat it up, wrapped in tin foil for 5-8 minutes in a hot oven or give it a quick burst, unwrapped, in a microwave.

To make the sauce heat the two ingredients together in a saucepan to a temperature of 240 degrees (soft ball) stirring occasionally. Serve hot but not boiling.

A small variation is to put in one teaspoonful of black treacle to create a darker sauce.

CREME BRULEE

To serve 6

1pt/600ml double cream
6 egg yolks
5oz/150grms castor sugar
a vanilla pod

Equipment 6 individual size ramekins

Preparation
Preheat the oven to No. 1/275 degrees

Method
Firstly to make the creamy custard, place the egg yolks with 2oz of the sugar in a deep bowl. In a small saucepan heat the cream with the vanilla pod until boiling. Remove the vanilla pod and pour on to the waiting eggs and sugar whisking all the time.

The next task is to pour the custard in to the ramekins, bearing in mind that there must be enough space left at the top for a layer of sugar.

Place the ramekins in a roasting tin and surround with hot water to come half way up. Place in the middle of the oven for 45 minutes – 1 hour or until the custards are set but not coloured. Allow to cool.

Light the grill and spread a teaspoonful of sugar over the top of each ramekin before putting under the grill for long enough to turn the sugar in to a crisp golden topping.

Serve warm or preferably chill for a short time.

APRICOT CLAFOUTIS

Clafoutis is of a deliciously soft consistency – almost a cross between egg custard and batter. It can be made with any fruit but is particularly good with apricots.

To serve 6-8

1lb/450grms poached or tinned apricots
$\frac{3}{4}$pt/450ml single cream
2 eggs
2oz/50grms castor sugar
1$\frac{1}{2}$oz/40grms plain flour
a measure of brandy
a pinch of salt

Equipment A ceramic flan dish – 10in. diameter and 1$\frac{1}{2}$in deep.

Preparation
Preheat the oven to No. 5/375 degrees

Method
It is aesthetically most pleasing to make this in a ceramic rather than a metal flan dish.

Quite simply arrange the apricots over the base of the dish and sprinkle over the brandy (cognac or apricot brandy). Now mix one of the eggs with the flour to a smooth paste. Add the other egg and stir together with the cream, sugar and salt. Gently pour over the apricots and bake in the middle of the oven for 35-40 minutes until firm to the touch.

Serve warm sprinkled with a little castor sugar, accompanied by cream.

BRANDIED FRUITS with CREME BRULEE

This is worth making in a reasonable quantity as it keeps well in a sealed jar (indeed it improves with keeping). Although it goes with all sorts of things it is particularly good with Creme Brulée, the recipe for which we give below.

6lbs/3 kilos dried mixed fruit to include pears, apple rings, prunes, apricots, peaches.
2 handfuls of raisins
2 oranges
1 bottle of sweet sherry
$\frac{1}{4}$ bottle of brandy
cold tea

The ideal containers for this are sweet jars as they are screw top, cheap and look attractive in the kitchen when filled. One jar holds 4lbs/2 kilos.

Start by cutting the zest from the oranges in to thin strips and mixing with all the dried fruit and raisins. Pack in to the jars and pour on the juice of the oranges, the brandy and the sherry. Top up with cold tea. Screw the lid on tightly, give the whole lot a shake and leave to stand for at least a week.

STRAWBERRY CHEESE TART

To serve 6-8

1½lbs/675grms perfect strawberries
1lb/450grms cream cheese
12oz/350grms shortcut pastry, see page 92
2oz/50grms castor sugar
¼pt/150ml single cream
3 tablespoonfuls of redcurrant jelly

Equipment A flan tin – 10in. diameter x 1in. deep

Preparation
Preheat the oven to No. 5/375 degrees
Lightly grease the flan tin.
Line the greased flan tin with the thinly rolled out pastry.
Prick all over with a fork and bake blind until crisp and golden. Allow to cool.

Method
This is very simple to prepare. The cream cheese is beaten together with the single cream and sugar and is spread over the base of the flan. The strawberries are arranged on the top and the whole thing is given an attractive glaze by spooning over melted redcurrant jelly.

TERRINE OF FRUIT

A colourful terrine of soft and exotic fruit set in a lemon mousse.

To serve 8

**8oz/225grms plain Victoria
sponge cake
a large measure of brandy
8oz/225grms large sound
strawberries
6 kiwi fruit
1 large ripe mango**

**THE MOUSSE
2 lemons
1½ sachets of Davis powdered
gelatine
3 eggs
½pt/300ml double cream**

Equipment A 4-4½pt/2.4-2.7 litres capacity loaf tin or terrine dish

Preparation
Line the base of the tin with greaseproof paper.
Peel the kiwi fruit and cut in half lengthways.
Peel the mango and cut the flesh away from the stone in large strips.
Remove the stems from the strawberries.

Method for the mousse
In this recipe we start by making the beginnings of an egg custard in to which
we whisk beaten egg whites and whipped cream to make a mousse.

First put a large saucepan of water on to boil. Next separate the eggs putting
the yolks in a china mixing bowl with the juice and zest from the lemons, the
sugar and the powdered gelatine. Place this bowl over the simmering water and
cook, whisking all the time until the mixture begins to thicken. Remove from the
heat and wait until it is cool and beginning to set.

Meanwhile whip the egg whites and the cream in separate bowls. Now fold the
cream and egg whites in to the yolk and sugar mixture. Keep at room
temperature.

Assembly
Line the tin with ¼in. layer cut from the sponge and sprinkle with brandy.

The amount of work you wish to put in to the assembly from now on is up to
you. You can be quite basic about it and simply stir all the fruits in to the
mousse and spoon in until the terrine is full.

If on the other hand you want to make it look really pretty when cut in to slices
you can put in a layer of mousse and then fruit and so on ending with a layer of
mousse.

Fit a final layer of sponge across the top, sprinkled with brandy and put the
terrine in the fridge to set overnight.

Turn out and cut in ¾ inch thick slices.

ICE CREAM

BASIC INGREDIENTS
4 eggs
3oz/75grms castor sugar
1pt/600ml double cream

An awful lot of unnecessary mystique has been built up in people's minds about the business of making ice cream at home. Contraptions that whirl in one's ice box, curious alpine looking wooden buckets with handles on the sides and so on. All are unnecessary with this delightfully simple recipe which produces delicious ice cream every time without fail.

The base to which you add any flavour that you like is made by taking two bowls and in one beating together the sugar and eggs until white and in the other whipping the cream until stiff.

Now simply combine the two, add the flavours and pour in to a polythene box and freeze for 24hrs.

SOME SUGGESTED FLAVOURINGS TO ADD TO THE PLAIN ICE CREAM

BANOFFI ICE CREAM
1 large tin of condensed milk
1 teaspoonful of powdered instant coffee
1 teaspoonful of freshly ground coffee
3 bananas

Boil the unopened, unpunctured tin of condensed milk in water for 3hrs. *making sure that the tin is at all times covered with water.* Lift out and allow to cool. Inside you have the most delicious toffee mixture which when mashed with the bananas and coffee will impart to your ice cream the same flavour that has made Banoffi Pie (see *Deeper Secrets of The Hungry Monk*, page 81) a household word.

CHERRY BRANDY ICE CREAM
1lb/450grms Tiptree Morello Cherry jam
5fl oz/125ml cherry brandy

Simply combine the ingredients and add to the plain ice cream mixture. This can be thoroughly mixed or half mixed to leave streaks.

PRALINE AND RAISIN ICE CREAM
12oz/350grms praline, see page 96
2 tablespoonfuls of soaked raisins, see page 94

Simply combine the praline and the raisins and stir in to the plain ice cream mixture.

CHOCOLATE LIQUEUR ICE CREAM
4oz/100grms Cadbury's plain Bournville Chocolate
7fl oz/175ml your favourite liqueur – we recommend Creme de Menthe, Tia Maria, Benedictine, Cointreau or Brandy.

Grate the chocolate in to chips and stir in to the plain ice cream followed by the liquor.

MISCELLANEOUS

BARBECUE SAUCE

For Pork, Duck and Kebabs

Ingredients for 1 pt/600ml

$\frac{3}{4}$pt/450ml Espagnole Sauce   Brown Sauce (See page 88)
the juice of two lemons
1 tablespoon of ready made English mustard
2 tablespoons of mango chutney
1 large pinch of cayenne pepper or chili powder
salt

Method
Simply combine all the ingredients in a pan and bring gently to the boil. Season to taste.

BEARNAISE SAUCE

For Steaks, Chicken and Fish

Ingredients for ½pt/300ml

8oz/225grms salted butter
the juice of two lemons
4fl oz/12ml dry white wine or dry sherry
3 egg yolks
1 shallot
1 teaspoon of black peppercorns
a sprig of fresh tarragon

Method
Finely chop the shallot. Boil the lemon juice and the wine together with the tarragon, peppercorns and shallot until reduced by half. This now becomes the basis when strained for the bearnaise. Transfer to a bains-marie, return to a low heat and blend in the egg yolks with a whisk, continuing until the mixture becomes thick and slightly foaming. Remove from the heat as it is crucial not to overcook at this stage. We are now ready to introduce the melted butter. This should be done by pouring it in as a thin stream, whisking vigorously. You will notice a white residue at the bottom of the butter – let this go in to the bearnaise. There should be no need for further seasoning. Set aside, keeping the sauce at kitchen temperature. Serve as soon as possible.

* If the sauce should separate follow the instructions on page 90

BECHAMEL SAUCE

This sauce forms the basis of a number of white sauces. The recipe is a little different from that shown in our other books as it has been designed specifically for the dishes in this book.

Ingredients for 2pts/1.2 litres

2pts/1.2 litres milk
1 onion coarsely chopped
3oz/85grms butter
3oz/85grms plain flour
$\frac{1}{2}$ a chicken stock cube – crumbled
3 bay leaves
2 cloves
salt and white pepper

Method

Heat the milk with the bay leaves, cloves, stock cube and onion. In a separate saucepan melt the butter and stir in the flour to form a roux. Next pour on the hot milk, whisking all the time and bring to the boil. Simmer for 5 minutes. Pass the entire mixture through a sieve and set aside.

If you are able to allow the Bechamel to stand this will both improve the flavour and increase the thickness.

BROWN SAUCE
(often referred to as Espagnole Sauce)

A good brown sauce is not dissimilar to a very full flavoured soup. This sauce forms the basis of a number of meat sauces. The recipe is a little different from that shown in our other books as it has been designed specifically for the dishes in this book.

Ingredients for 2pts/1.2 litres

2pts/1.2 litres brown stock
3oz/85grms good dripping
3oz/85grms plain flour
4oz/100grms tomato purée
1 small onion
1 small carrot
1 stick of celery
1oz/25grms streaky bacon
a few mushroom stalks if available
2 bay leaves
a pinch of mixed herbs
salt and freshly ground black pepper

Preparation
Roughly chop the onion, carrot, celery, mushroom stalks and bacon.

Method
Melt the dripping and add all the chopped ingredients together with the herbs, bay leaves, salt and pepper and fry until the vegetables are golden. Lower the heat, stir in the flour and cook for a few moments before gradually introducing the tomato puree and stock. Bring to the boil, stirring all the time and allow to simmer for a few minutes. Adjust the seasoning and enrich the colour with gravy browning if necessary.

Pass through a sieve in to a suitable storage container and set aside. If you are able to allow the sauce to stand this will improve the flavour and increase the thickness.

CHORON SAUCE

For Chicken, Fish and Vegetables

Ingredients for ½pt/300ml

½pt/300ml Bearnaise Sauce – see page 86
2 heaped tablespoons of peeled, seeded and chopped tomatoes.
salt
freshly ground black pepper

Method
Simply fold the the prepared tomatoes in to the bearnaise and adjust the seasoning to taste.

HOLLANDAISE SAUCE

Although Hollandaise is the base of all the sauces in this section it differs from the other hot base sauces in this book in that it is perfect on its own with almost any meat, fish or vegetable. It is particularly good with food cooked in pastry.

Ingredients for ½pt/300ml

8oz/grms salted butter
the juice of two lemons
3 egg yolks
half a teaspoon of French mustard

Method
This is a simple method of making a light creamy hollandaise using lemon juice and mustard rather than the more traditional reduction of vinegar with a bay leaf.

Start by thoroughly melting the butter, taking care not to brown it at all.

Next combine the egg yolks, lemon juice and mustard in the top half of a double saucepan away from the heat. Then place over the heat and whisk until thick and smooth (not scrambled!)

Transfer this in to an earthenware mixing bowl ready for the melted butter to be poured on in a thin stream, whisking all the time. The finished article should be smooth, creamy and shining with no sign of separation. There should be no need for further seasoning. Set aside keeping the sauce at kitchen temperature. Serve as soon as possible.

If the sauce should separate:- Do not be dismayed! Simply return the mixture to the heat in a double saucepan and bring up to a temperature hotter than blood heat but less than boiling. Take a clean bowl and fill it with boiling water — this warms the bowl. Pour off the hot water leaving a teaspoonful in the bottom. Now simply pour the separated hollandaise in a very fine stream on to the water whisking continuously. There are other methods of retrieving hollandaise but this way is fool proof.

To reheat leftover sauce:- Follow the instructions above.

MAYONNAISE

This recipe produces a delicious plain mayonnaise that is in itself full of flavour and quite suitable with any salad, cold fish or cold meat.

Ingredients for 1pt/600ml

1 pint/600ml pure vegetable oil *or condensed milk, vinegar to taste*
2 egg yolks
the juice of two lemons
1 tablespoon of ready made mustard
$\frac{1}{2}$ teaspoon of freshly ground black pepper
$\frac{1}{2}$ teaspoon of salt

Method

In cold weather take a double saucepan and warm the oil to blood heat. Place the egg yolk in a mixing bowl and blend in the mustard together with a little salt and pepper. It is necessary to alternately beat in small quantities of the oil until the mixture becomes very thick and then thin it down with the lemon juice. Continue this process, maintaining an even consistency until all the oil has been absorbed. The final consistency is a matter of taste and can simply be regulated by adding larger or smaller amounts of lemon juice. Adjust the seasoning.

The mayonnaise will keep indefinitely if kept in a properly sterilised air-tight jar.

If the Mayonnaise separates:- Stop! There is nothing for it but to start all over again with clean dry utensils. Separate an egg and place the yolk in a bowl. Pour on the broken mayonnaise mixture in a very fine stream whisking continuously. Once it has begun to emulsify the stream can be accelerated.

BROWN PASTRY

8oz/225grms plain white flour
2oz/50grms brown wholemeal flour
4oz/100grms butter
cold water
a pinch of salt

Method

Sieve the two sorts of flour with the salt in to a bowl. Cut the butter in to pieces and rub in to the flour until the consistency resembles fine breadcrumbs. Trickle in a little cold water, folding the mixture over with a knife until you have achieved a smooth dough. Set aside to relax for a least 30 minutes before using.

RICH SHORTCRUST PASTRY

We have found this pastry ideal for quiches and tarts as it moulds easily in to the flan tin, bakes really crisply and in using more than half fat to flour we prevent shrinkage when baking blind.

8oz/225grms plain flour
5oz/150grms butter
1 egg
cold water
a pinch of salt

Method

Sieve the flour with the salt in to a bowl. Cut the butter in to pieces and rub in to the flour until the consistency of fine breadcrumbs has been achieved. Make a well in the centre of the flour and first crack the egg in to this followed by as much water as half of the eggshell holds. Work with the fingertips to a smooth dough.

Variation

HAZELNUT PASTRY

3oz/75grms hazelnuts

To remove the skins, roast the nuts on a tray in a No.3/325 degrees oven for 20 minutes and after allowing to cool, roll them between the palms of your hands. Crush the nuts in a mortar and pestle and stir in to the flour before making the pastry.

PANCAKES

To make 12 Pancakes

4oz/100grms plain flour
3 eggs
8fl oz/225ml milk
2 tablespoonfuls of vegetable oil
salt

First the pan. Avoid anything with too steep a sides. If it is not already non-stick you can make it so by heating some salt in it and wiping out with a dry cloth.

In this recipe we incorporate a little oil in the batter so that the pancakes are self-lubricating.

Make the batter by whisking together the flour, eggs, salt and a little of the milk in to a thick smooth paste. Add the rest of the milk and a tablespoonful of the oil. Allow to stand for 30 minutes.

Lightly coat the pan with the remaining tablespoonful of oil, draining off any excess. Pour in enough mixture to thinly cover the base and cook over a high flame for about 10 seconds easing the edges with a palette knife. Turn the pancake and give a further 5 seconds. Turn out on to a plate. Repeat the process until all the batter is used. The oil in the batter allows you to stack the pancakes on top of each other without risk of them sticking together.

BREADCRUMBS

For savoury dishes

8oz/335grms stale bread – with any dark crusts removed
2oz/50grms porridge oats
1 level dessertspoonful of Herbes de Provence
1 dessertspoonful of chopped parsley
salt and freshly ground black pepper

Simply break up the bread and liquidise with all the other ingredients. This will keep indefinitely if stored in a loosely covered container in a dry corner of the kitchen.

DUXELLE STUFFING

1lb/450grms white button mushrooms – wiped and sliced
1 medium-sized onion – finely chopped
2oz/50grms butter
1 teaspoonful of Moutarde de Meaux
the juice of $\frac{1}{2}$ a lemon
1 pinch of Herbes de Provence
salt and freshly ground black pepper

Melt the butter in a pan and cook the onions until soft. Toss in the mushrooms, herbs, salt and pepper and continue to cook until the juice from the mushrooms has reduced to nothing. Stir in the mustard and lemon juice and transfer the whole mixture to a liquidiser. Pulverise to a puree and store in the fridge.

As a variation some anchovy fillets can be added before pureeing to give a very useful stuffing for eggs or spread on croutes as a short eat with drinks.

SOAKED RAISINS

No cook should be without a little jar of raisins soaking away in a mixture of sherry, brandy, wine or any other unfinished booze, ready to be tossed in to anything from bread and butter pudding, spotted dick and fruit cake to home-made ice cream or the Chocolate Praline Slice shown on page 94

BLOCK ROUX

There are a number of sauces in this book, where it is much easier to make the roux as you go. However, there are occasions when a block of ready-made roux can usefully be grated and whisked into a stock or sauce to thicken it.

Ingredients
Equal quantities of butter or margarine and plain white flour.

Method
Take a heavy-based saucepan and heat the butter until bubbling but not browned. Stir in the flour using a wooden spoon and continue stirring over a medium flame for about two minutes before proceeding with the particular sauce recipe you have chosen to make.

Block Roux
Remove the roux from the heat and whilst it is still warm, spoon it into an earthenware jar or bowl to set. Once set you can turn it out of the container and wrap it in greaseproof paper or foil to be kept in the refrigerator.

CLARIFIED BUTTER

To attain pure unsalted butter oil which is capable of being cooked to much hotter temperatures without browning. Melt the butter in a small saucepan and heat until foaming. Skim off the surface scum with a ladle and pour the remains in to a bowl and chill. Any remaining sediment will sink to the bottom and may thus be easily separated.

PRALINE

Apart from being used in two recipes in this book (page 73-82) this is good stuff to have around. Sprinkled on to anything it adds interest particularly to trifles, syllabubs, cold souffles, etc.

4oz/100grms hazelnuts
4oz/100grms blanched almonds
1lb/450grms granulated sugar
$\frac{1}{4}$pt/150ml water

Roast the nuts on a tray in the middle of a No. 3/325 degrees oven for 15-20 minutes until golden. At the same time boil the sugar and water together until they carmelise (380 degrees) and show a deep golden colour. Pour the caramel over the nuts on to an oiled marble slab or baking tray. Allow to go crack hard and pound to a granular consistency. This stores in an airtight jar indefinitely.

Dips – for Chips   Helena –

1 tin condensed milk.
Tomato sauce

NOTES